MW01147716

girl, isolated

also by trista mateer

The Dogs I Have Kissed

Honeybee

Aphrodite Made Me Do It

When the Stars Wrote Back

SAPPHIC
HEARTBREAK

HEALING
NOTES
FROM THE
UNIVERSE

MYTHIC
SELF
CARE +
THOUGHTS
ON LOVE

MESSY
UGLY
INTIMACY
ISSUES

content warning

This book contains explicit language as well as sensitive material related to the following:

mental health/depression and anxiety
suicide/suicidal ideation
self-harm
fire
death
violence
disordered eating
emotional abuse
substance use/alcohol mention
pandemic/sickness/discussion of covid-19

girl,

isolated

poems, reflections, various lonelinesses,
notes on resilience, and so on...

trista
mateer

ISBN: 9798746574596

Cover and interior design by Trista Mateer

For any inquiries please don't hesitate to get in touch.
tristamateerpoetry.com/contact

for you and whatever gets you through

THESE PAGES WERE WRITTEN BETWEEN
MARCH 2020 AND MARCH 2021

INT. BEDROOM — NIGHT

POET (twenties, American, unshowered) rubs
her eyes and gets out of bed for the first
time today.

She crosses the room to turn on the light.
Now her messy living space is in full view.
Wine bottle propped against a pile of dirty
laundry. Ashes on the dresser. An empty
cereal box on the nightstand. Dishes stacked
on the floor. The fitted sheet is peeling
back off the bed.

She spies the bottle, turns the light off,
and climbs back into bed with the wine.

The phone rings.

She hesitates for a long moment before
clearing her throat and answering it.

                POET
     Hi. Hello.

                MUSE
     Hey. Is this a bad time?

                POET
     Yes.

to my ex-lover during quarantine

I hope your baby is safe but I still don't give a rat's ass about your husband / what I mean is / I hope there is always toilet paper in your house / I hope you still go outside to feel the sun but I also hope everyone stays six feet away from you / I hope your hands are clean / it has not been long enough since I last thought of you / but of course I am thinking of you now / of course I am / I am back in the town where we fell in love and every place we used to go is closed / I don't wish you were here but I wish you weren't in San Diego / I wish you someplace quieter / forgive me for caring / forgive me for writing this poem / forgive me for ripping my eyes away from the news long enough to write anything at all

lonely is lonelier
when you say it out loud
and I'd swear by that

when I'm not checking
to see if someone texted me
I'm waiting to check

passing time until I can
look at the phone once again
hoping I just missed the buzz

I COULD PASS ~~THE~~ MY TIME WITHOUT YOU
I COULD WRITE LESS POEMS ABOUT YOU
I COULD JUST FORGET YOUR FAVORITE THINGS
I COULD HARDEN UP MY HEART
ACCEPT THAT WE'LL STAY MILES APART
PUT DOWN THE FUCKING TELEPHONE
EACH TIME IT RINGS

BUT I WON'T
I'M TOO STONED
I HATE BEING HOME ALONE
I HATE THIS HOUSE I HATE THIS COUCH
I HATE MYSELF

I HATE BEING HERE WITHOUT YOU
EVEN THOUGH I'VE GROWN TO DOUBT YOU
AND THE ONLY ONE I BLAME HERE
IS MYSELF

SO I WON'T
I'M TOO STONED
I HATE BEING HOME ALONE
I'LL PLAY THE FOOL IF IT'S AN INTERESTING PART
YOU'RE ALWAYS A GREAT DISTRACTION
EVEN WHEN THERE IS NO ACTION
AND I GUESS IF I GET SAD
I'LL MAKE SOME ART

Yes, this March is a shitstorm
but there will still be next March
and the one after that.
Maybe not for me
but for someone;
and I can still find that beautiful for a moment
before I beg for my own bad lungs.

excerpts

I know the whole world feels like it's on fire but it's not. Well, parts of it are not. Well, [...] I love you enough to stay away from you [...] but on the other hand, I would fight giant murder hornets to see you right now. And I might have to [...] it's true. The restaurant where we fell in love is closed to the public but they still offer delivery [...] Call anytime. Day or night. [...] Call anytime [...] Call when you can [...] call if you can. [...] We're going to be okay again one day and I will hold you until then. [...] or I would [...] if I could! There are so many things I would do if I could do them right now. [...] Remind me why we live on opposite sides of the country again? [...] remind me of anything at all. [...] Remember the summer we drove your car across the US and [...] what if we never get to do anything like that again? [...] remember when we were twenty-four and [...] almost never thought about dying? [...] My mother is fighting with me again about the news but I think I can slip away for a minute to talk if you're free. [...] remember being free? [...] No, but I'm disappointed anyway. [...] I'm having a hard time but I guess everyone is [...] so I no longer fear being unloved [...] at the end of the world. [...] I wish I had less people [...] to love. [...] My heart feels like it's beating out of my chest.

I'VE BEEN HAVING SOME TROUBLE
GETTING OUT OF BED

NEEDED NEW REASONS
NOT TO WASTE THE DAY INSTEAD

SO I BOUGHT A FEW PLANTS
TO FILL THE HOLE INSIDE MY HEAD

AND NOW I WAKE TO WATER
WHAT I DON'T WANT DEAD

so yes
I'm writing some poems
and no
they aren't masterful or even good really
I'm writing them anyway
I am writing bad poems but I am writing
look at that
all the things I can still do even when I'm grieving
who can blame themselves for not being prolific
during panic
the good poems will come later
god willing
and everyone will just have to wait

incomplete list of reasons i cried today

the news was on
the news is always on
I can't escape the news
I saw an article about a stranger's death
and it left me feeling empty
I don't know if I want the right things
I don't know if I want the same things I used to want
I don't really feel very safe at all
it's an uncomfortable time to be alive
it's an uncomfortable time to be anything
I looked at my bank account
shouldn't have looked at my bank account
I don't know how to make people care about other people
empathy is Missing In Action MIA
my childhood best friend is a bigot now
my hometown
the way it keeps spitting me out
but here we are
here we are
here we still are
and my career is in shambles
if you can even call it a career
and well yeah my hair is going gray
and I'm unloved
and I'm nearing the end of my twenties
and the world seems so unpromising
the taste is off
like all the goodness left is at the bottom of the cup
and we're sipping from the top
without stirring

I CAN FEEL MYSELF UNRAVELING
LIKE A BALL OF YARN ROLLING
ACROSS THE LIVING ROOM FLOOR

I'M SPINNING OUT

RIGHT IN FRONT OF EVERYONE

titles of poems i'm too tired to write

WHAT IF IT DOESN'T GET BETTER THAN
THIS (WHAT IF THIS IS IT)

I NEED TO BELIEVE IN SOMETHING GOOD
SO I'M BELIEVING IN POETRY AGAIN

EVERYTHING REMINDS ME OF WHAT I
DON'T WANT TO REMEMBER

IF I IGNORE THOSE BILLS THEY MIGHT GO
AWAY (AND OTHER LIES I TELL MYSELF AT
NIGHT)

I CAN FEEL MY HEART GETTING HARDER
AS WE SPEAK / IT HAS TO / HOW ELSE DO
YOU SURVIVE

I grew my nails out in April
filed and shaped meticulously for days
until they were perfect

and then I bit them off.
There's a metaphor in there somewhere
but I don't feel like being introspective enough
to figure it out.

Grant me the wisdom
to not assess my flaws during quarantine.

Good god
          don't I at least
          deserve   that much

          of a break ?

the part of my brain that fears love, speaks

All people want to do is trap you.
That's what love is.
The hesitation before leaving.
Love   is a long pause
before breaking a neck. A long con.
A big cat and mouse game.
People just want to take in an unloved thing
and make it good again.
Let it enjoy the heat and the food.
Let it get comfortable.
Until they run off
to find the next unloved thing.

You're not gonna catch me inside again.
I'll snap at anything that bleeds

just to get it the fuck away from   me.

MUSE
You are still hurt by the oldest
wounds. Don't you let anything
heal?

POET
I'd rather hold a grudge than
have an empty hand. At least it's
something.

I'm still crying over
that Taylor song
and all the love
that's done me wrong

I'll hold onto anything at night
when I'm lonely

i'm sorry for looking you up online

I wanted to see if your face still looks the way I remember it. And it does. And it doesn't. You look softer, happier. All those hard edges worn away. No more crying on coke and fucking strangers from the internet. No more late night phone calls.

We all file down our claws eventually. It's to be expected. We leave our ugliness in locked rooms and learn to play nice.

So it's my own fault. Of course it is. Being here and seeing this. And it's not that I'm upset that you're married. It's that it's hard to imagine a hand that's been around my throat doing the kinds of things that married hands do.

I can see it, you know. The other life with the worse decisions. Some lost version of me taking her place. Sitting prim and pretty by your side during the daytime. Holding your hand in Facebook photos. No more snarl. No more dirt. No more showing up on your street at 2am after drinking a fishbowl of vodka and letting you crumple my body like a candy wrapper.

But you wanted to choke on something sweet. What was I supposed to do? You wanted me to save you. So we played god for a little while. Now we don't play anything at all.

You touched me more than once with tenderness and I never mistook it for affection. I know the code of miserable people. I was the rat trap for your loneliness. And the rat. And the loneliness.

See how much poison I can swallow when it's hand-fed?

I CAN'T TELL IF I MISS TEXAS
OR IF I MISS YOUR FACE
I JUST KNOW I WON'T SEE EITHER
IF I'M STUCK STANDING IN PLACE
AND I DON'T WANNA BE HERE
BUT THAT DON'T MEAN I NEED YOUR ARMS
AND I'M SURE CALLING UP TO TALK IT OUT
WOULD ONLY CAUSE US HARM

texts from an unknown number

Tuesday 2:17 AM

i've had six shots of whiskey and i miss your face
remember last year when you came to my place?
i kissed your thighs and i pulled at your waist
and then when you left well i guess i just spaced
i should have called then but i'm calling now
well not calling per se but i'm reaching out
i wanted to know if you had any doubts
and if not then that's fine but i miss you
and if not then that's fine but i wish i could kiss you
i'm holed up at home and i'm sad and alone
and i'm just sitting here with my dick and my phone
the world is so bleak and i'm well past my peak
and i'm terrified nobody wants me

3:12 AM

anyway i guess this came out of the blue
and i'm lonely yeah but don't think i need you
i don't even know why i bothered to text
i mean you're not even my prettiest ex
and i loved other girls more than i liked you

1:38 PM

you're a bitch for not answering
i'm glad that we're through

Thursday 11: 46 PM

fuck you

If there is a universe parallel to ours where time moves backwards, then that means I blinked into existence already in love with you there. That means things there remind me of you and I still don't know why but one day I will. One day I will, because there is still a future there for us.

I am running toward a future there where we will collide brilliantly one day and everything will make sense all of a sudden. Why I already knew the sound of your laugh. Why your name made me ache before I even met you. There will be time for us even if it's backwards.

We will love each other very much and then be friends for a long time after that and then one day I'll wake up and not remember you at all.

Which is to say, maybe that universe is a kinder one or at least a place where it is easier to let go. Because there I will forget, and here I have to carry love with me quietly forever.

oh goddamn
I sent a text I swore I wouldn't
it said, *I fucking miss you*
even when I know I shouldn't

housecat
circling the foot of my bed,
threadbare walls and the shouting downstairs,
plants drying out on the sill. Just   like   me,
uprooted on the floor
trying to take in all this wide open plainness.
television episodes streaming on for miles.
I did open the windows for the first time in months.
all this new American wilderness
and still nowhere to get lost.

In the spring of our worst year,
I made cakes every day

like I was celebrating being alive.
It didn't last. Got sad and mean

in no time at all.

in lockdown, i spiral effortlessly

the thing about Tiger King is that I know I'm not
supposed to root for that lady but I do anyway / haven't
we all wanted to feed a man to a Big Cat at some point /
and I'm sorry but I did watch every pandemic movie ever
made this year / and every email I get makes me want to
dissolve / like yeah maybe we'll just work straight on
through trauma and see how that goes / my hair is falling
out / maybe from stress / maybe not / and the news
cycles on / another name on the list of names / and
another name on the list of names / and another name
on the list of names / and another name on the list of
names / last night I put a t-shirt on one of my pillows /
fell asleep holding it / how do you categorize your specific
brand of lonely / I keep contacting the Neopets team
asking for my old account back and they won't respond /
I know I don't feel like myself but I'm starting to forget
what that felt like at all / it's not still March / but it's
March in spirit / all this talk of *acceptable losses* /
ambivalence in the face of mass suffering / say it again /
Black lives fucking matter / anti-Asian hate crimes are on
the rise / and the police care more about property than
people / it's true there was another suicide down the
street / and yes your ex-favorite childhood author is the
transphobic bigot of the year / things do get worse as
soon as you think they can't / I forget why I used to like
to leave the house / they showed someone murdered on
the news again / again / again / I am back in the shower
only this time there's wine / and blood too / What
Would Dolly Parton Do / the chest pains are back again /
everything is on fire but it feels impolite to scream about
it / everyone thinks the news is wild right now but I don't
think it will ever go back to normal /   how can it?

Good morning, it's Tuesday.
Or maybe it's not. I threw out the calendar,

shredded my day planner, tired of
being mocked by its emptiness.

you're not alone in the way you are feeling
you're not alone in the way you are feeling
you're not alone in the way you are feeling

You're not alone in the way you are feeling. I repeat this to myself nightly. Awake in the dark I speak into the empty room. I say, *listen to me. I know you feel like the last person on the planet but you're not. There are signs of life out there. Things are going to grow again.*

I can feel it happening. I can feel my aloneness making
me a stranger. I can feel my aloneness making me a
weirder person. Unchecked habits and sweatpants.
Oversharing to anyone who will listen for longer than two
minutes. Voice messages all the time instead of texts

because

well, because you might respond with one too and then I
get to listen to something other than the sound of myself.

I'll do anything if you say my name three times.

I need to be reminded that I exist.

small ghost plays animal crossing

spends hours and hours
        hours and hours
        hours and hours
rearranging an untouchable house because
she   knows

there will never be an opportunity for her
to have a real home
to belong to a real place

so she puts in her time
builds all her furniture, trades for nothing
cleans up the beaches every day
checks in on her neighbors
feels
        something like relief

when she realizes this virtual island
might be the last beautiful thing she ever creates

small ghost communicates with the living

or, she tries to

she bangs the pots and pans together
she dumps the laundry on the floor
she lights every candle in the house
she just wants someone to look at her again

You could just kill yourself instead,
she thinks.

She hates herself for thinking it.

Wouldn't have to hate yourself
if you were dead, though
her brain counters.

live photo

My grandmother brings me her phone
and says,   *look.*

The lock screen is a photo
of the dog she had to put down
a few months ago. *I miss him
so much,* she says.

She presses her finger to the image
until it comes to life for approximately
three seconds   and says,

look   it's like he's breathing again.

I wonder if one day
someone will do that to a photo of me.

trista mateer

MUSE
I don't think you're ready to
write about it.

POET
I'm not. But what else is there
to do inside this room?

MUSE
It's going to come out wrong.

POET
But it's going to come out.

grief for who I have lost
grief for who you have lost
grief for the world
grief for what life was before this
grief for what life will be after this
grief for all the old grief
grief for all the new grief
grief for what has been missed
grief for what has been ruined
grief for distance
grief for the expanse of solitude
grief for grief's sake
grief for life, upended

I THINK IT'S POSSIBLE
TO GET STUCK INSIDE YOURSELF
TO EAT YOURSELF ALIVE
AND JUST FORGET TO ASK FOR HELP

grief like a summer storm
  sudden

grief like wine from the bottle
     an outpouring

grief like grief like grief like grief

google search: other words for grief

grief just sounds right though doesn't it?
a thing you could wrap around the shoulders
and forget to take off

grief and grief and grief on the body

not like a wave
but still grief like an ocean
I'm too scared to explore how deep it goes
I don't wanna know what's down there

THE WORLD FEELS LIKE IT'S ENDING
OF COURSE I AM CALLING YOU

I BARELY HESITATED AT ALL

I AM CALLING BECAUSE I LOVE YOU

I AM CALLING BECAUSE PEOPLE ARE DYING
AND ONE DAY YOU COULD BE ONE OF THEM

I AM CALLING BECAUSE I STILL HAVE THINGS TO SAY

I AM CALLING BECAUSE I NEVER
THOUGHT I'D HAVE TO

THOUGHT YOU'D BE HERE ALREADY
HOLDING MY HAND
AND WATCHING THE SMOKE

so yes I got too high and I could feel my heartbeat in my mouth when you messaged me and my vision went fuzzy for a minute / I love you so much it makes me see the wrong colors / and I needed that / I needed a feeling to hold onto / I needed a god to believe in and it couldn't be me this time / it couldn't be god either obviously / so it's you / I feel like my world is cracking down the middle and you are the glue holding shit together / you are the only joy I can feel in my throat / I need texts from you right now like I need water / I hate this part of myself because she's so fucking sweet on you / I do / I can say that and have it be true and still be in love with you / it's not that I don't want to need you / it's that I don't want to need anybody

AT THE END IT'S
GOING TO BE ME ~~AND~~
~~YOU~~ NO MATTER WHAT

GIRL, GOING THROUGH IT. GIRL, ALONE. GIRL, UNDER-COVERS. GIRL, IN ABSOLUTE HYSTERICS. GIRL, DISILLUSIONED. GIRL, WREAKING HAVOC. GIRL, JUST MAKING A MESS OF THINGS. GIRL, GHOSTING. GIRL, HAUNTING. GIRL, UNABLE TO RUN AWAY FROM HER PROBLEMS. GIRL, DISTANCED FROM HERSELF. GIRL, LOSING IT A LITTLE. GIRL, UNDER WRAPS. GIRL, UNDISCOVERED. GIRL, ABSENT. GIRL, VICIOUS. GIRL, WISHING VICIOUS WISHES. GIRL, COVERING THE MIRRORS. GIRL, OVERLY CAUTIOUS. GIRL, NOT CAUTIOUS ENOUGH. GIRL, IN THE THICK OF IT. GIRL, IN THE WOODS. GIRL, NEVER GETTING OUT OF HERE. GIRL, RECLUSIVE. GIRL, RUBBING HER SKIN RAW. GIRL, SO INSIDIOUS. GIRL, (YES) MALEVOLENT. GIRL, DESTROYING JUST TO HAVE SOMETHING TO TOUCH. GIRL, OF MADNESS AND RUINATION. GIRL, BLISTERED. GIRL, BLESSED. GIRL, UNFOLDED. GIRL, FUCKED UP. GIRL, NOT SO GIRL ALL THE TIME BUT DIGGING HER NAILS INTO THE TITLE NONETHELESS. GIRL, NEVER LETTING GO. GIRL, UNIDENTIFIED. GIRL, FERAL ON THE FLOOR. GIRL, CRYING IN THE SHOWER. GIRL, DRUNK ON HER OWN POWER. GIRL, PANTING HER OWN NAME. GIRL, GETTING THROUGH.

the wild thing

I used to treat my life like it was a little beast.
A wild thing chained outside,
always howling and yapping.
I ran with it for a while.
Let it loose in airports and other people's beds.
There was blood everywhere for a long time
but it got cold outside and I have a heart, you know.
I let it in.
Made a nest for it.
Coddled it.
Watched it grow fat and timid.
That was the end of wilderness tapping at my door.
I thought I was doing the right thing
but it still cries to go outside.
It sits by the windows when it thinks I'm not looking.
It has such sad eyes and it didn't always.
I'd let it back out but it's been so long.
It wouldn't know what to do out there.
It never uses its claws anymore.

despite this horrible year,
I still hope to look back and remember
our refusal to put down the phone,
the day we decided
to start writing emails to each other again
because we missed love letters,
the bread I baked
and how much I wanted to share it with you,
the sunlight lazy and warm
on my daily government allocated walk

Try to get some sun and water eventually.
Care for your body like it's a plant
if you can't care for it like it's a body.

I'm sorry. I don't know what else to say.
It's not really a good time for waxing poetic.

You are hurting and I cannot go to you.
Words do little to comfort in the absence of touch.

I wish I could hug you.
I wish I could breathe the air you are breathing.

I CAN'T REMEMBER
WHAT I MISS BUT I AM
MISSING SOMETHING
DEEPLY

THOUGHT IF I COULD PAINT YOUR FACE
FROM MEMORY
I COULD PROVE THAT NOTHING CHANGES
BUT ALL THE COLORS SEEM TO BLUR
AND THE BRUSH JUST REARRANGES
LINES AND STROKES
INTO FAMILIAR SHAPES

NOTHING REALLY LOOKS THE SAME
AS I REMEMBER IT

NOTHING MAKES ME FEEL
THE WAY THAT I REMEMBER IT

a dream

everyone you love is in the same room and they're standing less than six feet apart and the lights are off but no one is scared because everyone is singing happy birthday happy birthday and the cake is on its way out of the kitchen and your friends' faces are beaming and the candles are flickering and the icing is melting and everyone loves you so much and they're asking what you wish for and you're

choking on want

a wish

a hand on my face, some assurance that I exist outside of other people's perceptions of me, a voice calling my name from the dark saying you're so loved you're so loved you're so loved

I exist

you're so loved

I'm so loved...

Call me up
and ignore the smoke outside.

Call me up
and tell me about your day.

Make everything good again
with your own quiet goodness.

nursing my panic

today
i am sorrow walking, well
pacing, well
sitting on the edge of the bed
until i unfold into the shape of myself
pressed against the mattress
and what is there to mourn except every-
thing every
day? melancholia
is a weighted blanket
pulled up, tucked just
under the chin
harder to move now
but it sure is warm under here

so many bad things are happening
that it feels like no bad things are happening.

when everything is terrible
is anything really terrible?

what I mean is

how do you pile grief on top of other grief
and expect it to look different?

death means almost nothing
if you stare at it

long enough.

someone else I know just died

and

here I am thinking about Olive Garden
wondering if I could be more hungry
or more white

here I am binge-eating
and watching some show I've already seen
at least twice

here I am numb
and wasting what's left
of my own life

MUSE
Tell me what you want from this
restless life of yours.

POET
I can't. I don't know. The world
is a closed fist. All my options
are slipping away. I barely feel
connected to anything.

I DON'T KNOW WHY YOU'RE ASKING.
OF COURSE I WANNA RUN.
I PUT MY EGGS IN ONE BASKET,
THEN I BROKE THEM ONE BY ONE.
NOW I FIND THERE'S NOT MUCH LEFT HERE,
MESS THAT AIN'T WORTH MOPPING UP.
SO YEAH I WANNA RUN AGAIN
BUT I'M HOPING THAT WILL STOP.

I SWEAR TO GOD I AM TRYING TO SETTLE.
MY LEGS ARE TIRED AND I WANNA LIE DOWN.
I WON'T EVEN BE MAD TO GET STUCK IN THIS TOWN.

IT COULD BE WORSE.
AT LEAST YOU'RE STILL AROUND.

herculean

depression is a monster with many heads
and all of them are looking for me.

entire days
spent
staring
at the
veins
in my
wrists.

running
fingers
over
them.

wishing
i could
pluck
them
out.

wondering
what
they'd
look like
exposed
to
open
air.

sorry to interrupt your reading

We probably don't know each other but I hope you're happy. We might never speak but I hope you're doing okay. I'm just putting this out there in case the universe is listening. I hope everything works out for you.

I really hope it does.

I am writing to you now
because I am having a hell of a time

because I don't know what else to do

because the words are kindling
and the poem is a little fire
holding back the dark.

I'M SO FUCKING USELESS. I'M SO FUCKING LONELY. NOT SURE HOW TO SAY I NEED SOMEONE TO HOLD ME. AND MY MOTHER LIKES TO JOKE THAT I'M JEALOUS OF THE FAMILY DOG. CAN'T SEE THAT I JUST WANT TO BE A RECIPIENT OF MY PARENTS' LOVE. MY EX WAS PROBABLY RIGHT WHEN SHE TOLD ME I WOULD DIE ALONE. AND I'M ONLY A POET BECAUSE SHE LEFT ME WITH A POEM. I STILL DEFINE MY LIFE BY THE HURT IT'S PUT ME THROUGH AND THEN I ACT SURPRISED WHEN HURT IS ALL I SEEM TO DO. I'VE SPENT THE LAST DECADE LYING IN MY OWN WAY AND I STILL DON'T HAVE THE GUTS TO SAY HALF THE SHIT I NEED TO SAY.

Death comes around again
and I'm waiting this time.
Haven't had company in so long.
I'm beaming at the door.
I'm not shy about it,
so I ask Death to touch me.
A hand on the back.
Fingers wrapped lightly
around the wrist.
A brush of the arm.
Or more.
More is good.
Anything you want,
really.

I try to ~~write a poem about hope but~~

~~I try to write a poem~~

~~I try to write~~

I try

the poem is a conversation
and I am begging you to pause   here
and have it with me

I hope you're well
I understand

grab something to write with

* IN CASE NO ONE HAS ASKED LATELY

HOW ARE YOU DOING?

LIKE FOR REAL

hope, is alive. I'm still here. & I want to be. that can be enough

things that make me want to stay

the smell of freshly peeled citrus   meringues
     love in a broad and general sense

the Lord of the Rings soundtracks   good books

         the smell of the ocean
         the Chesapeake Bay

         the constant threat of new Taylor Swift songs
dnd podcasts   my friends' poetry

I don't know   other things probably
             neon motel signs   nearly-empty airports
sushi from that one place, do you remember?

             stubbornness and spite too
     mangos always   peaches and honey   making art

knowing that at least one thing I've written
has helped another person feel less alone

I do have big dreams for my life even though I'm always
     pretending I don't   small dreams too

Thrasher's Fries on the boardwalk
browned butter in the pan   I don't know   listen

I usually don't feel like I belong anywhere   but sometimes
     there's this glimmer of feeling like maybe I could

and I want to chase that   even if I never catch it

things that make you want to stay

your work making me feel less alone

dogs
family
friends

REMEMBER

THE GOOD DOESN'T HAVE TO OUTNUMBER THE BAD

IT JUST HAS TO BE THERE

give yourself permission to

CRY

STRUGGLE

SPEAK UP
SPEAK OUT

EAT

FUCK

EXPERIENCE
JOY

BE ANGRY

LOVE

REST

EXIST

HOPE

GRIEVE

CREATE

survive

CRY AGAIN

without guilt

JOURNAL OR POETRY PROMPT

PERSONIFY GRIEF OR LONELINESS AND
TELL ME ABOUT YOUR RELATIONSHIP.

ex. when Loneliness visits, it uses all the sugar
and sleeps in my bed.

my Grief is...
my loneliness is...
...my relationships are...

how do you
feel about
love these days?

POUR
YOUR
HEART
OUT

Every time I'm in the garden
I wish that I could bury
all the hurt I've trapped inside
that I still force myself to carry.

ADD ANOTHER STANZA -OR- TELL ME WHAT YOU NEED TO BURY

Shame

checking in
*please circle your answers

everything is
      a. just so much
      b. totally absolutely fine
      c. horrible

and i am
      a. handling it with grace
      b. barely holding it together
      c. fucking tired

and poetry is
      a. a welcome distraction
      b. making me feel better
      c. making me feel worse lol

ACB

JOURNAL PROMPT

How has this period of struggle
changed you? Have you had any
realizations about who you are
or who you want to be?

I'm still here
I am who I
want to be.

reader,

Thanks for being here. Really. This all could have been a lot worse for me. And I could have been alone really alone terrifyingly alone but I wasn't. I had you. And I knew you wouldn't answer for a long time. I knew the work of writing would be appropriately lonely. Months of quiet. But you're here now. You're here now. I'm so glad to meet you. I'm so happy to have someone to talk to. I wrote all of this for you. Don't laugh, I really did. Life's gone terribly off script and I wanted to tell you about it. I wanted to tell you everything.

THE SADNESS OF
HOMETOWNS

THE SADNESS OF
UNTIMELY DEATH

THE SADNESS OF
MISSING EVERYTHING
ALL AT ONCE

THE SADNESS OF
CONFRONTING YOUR PARENTS'
MORTALITY

THE SADNESS OF
WATCHING YOUR LIFE CHANGE
WITHOUT YOUR PERMISSION

THE SADNESS OF
STAGNANCY

THE SADNESS OF
NOT BEING ABLE TO SMILE
AT STRANGERS IN PUBLIC

THE SADNESS OF
LOST CONNECTION

THE SADNESS OF
LIFE'S CRUELTY
TRAUMA'S REIGN
GRIEF'S INEVITABLE RESURGENCE

HERE WE GO AGAIN

~~ALIVE~~

~~[illegible crossed-out text]~~

~~[illegible crossed-out text]~~

~~[illegible crossed-out text]~~

BUT YOU COME HOME FROM GOING OUT
AND YOU COUGH ON ME LIKE IT'S A JOKE.
THIS DOESN'T FEEL VERY MUCH
LIKE ANYBODY'S HOME.
YOU CHANGE YOUR FACE
IN THE MIDDLE OF A CONVERSATION.
YOU TELL ME THAT YOU LOVE ME
BUT YOU TREAT ME LIKE YOU FUCKING HATE ME.
~~EVERY TIME THE NEWS COMES ON~~
~~I HAVE TO RUN AND HIDE.~~
~~YOU NEED A VERBAL PUNCHING BAG~~
~~BUT I GUESS A DAUGHTER WORKS JUST FINE~~
~~IN THE MEANTIME.~~

And there is my mother, again
with her thin wrists buried in my trash.
Her ear pressed against my bedroom door.
Her eyes grazing on my privacy.
She hands me a journal from last year
and says, *maybe you want to look at page forty-seven*
where you resolved to be a kinder person.
Clearly you failed.
She's intrusive and correct.
But I am wrathful and reliably untamed
so I bite the hand that never fed me
and it hits back until I open my mouth.
Not too much blood,
but enough to point fingers.
I am the animal let loose in the house.
I am the barking bitch,
hackles raised at the television.

Hey team!

We know you are all feeling the effects of the current global pandemic, and

. We wish you and your loved ones a very

busy

lifetime.

Here are some tips on getting more done.

if you're struggling

please,

don't hesitate to talk to someone

else

I'm sorry. I should be getting more done.

I should be
getting
more
done

I should

I should be getting
more done.
I should be
I should be

essential work

They called you a hero
when they asked you to die.
It wasn't a war
but they called you frontline.
Thought if you had purpose
you wouldn't ask why
your life had been traded
for nickels and dimes.

*WHAT AM I SUPPOSED
TO DO WITH ALL THIS
INSATIABLE ANGER?*

*WHAT AM I SUPPOSED
TO DO WITH ALL THIS
INSATIABLE FEAR?*

*WHAT AM I SUPPOSED
TO DO WITH ALL THIS
INSATIABLE DESPAIR?*

A STRANGER DROPPED OFF MEDICINE AT MY DOOR
A TEXT FROM AN UNKNOWN NUMBER
LET ME KNOW IT WAS THERE, BEFORE
I TOOK THE FIRST STEP OUTSIDE I'D DONE IN MONTHS
I'M MORE LONELY THAN I EVER WAS

THE FIRST TIME I SPOKE TO SOMEONE ELSE THIS YEAR
WHO DOESN'T LIVE IN MY MOTHER'S HOUSE
OR INSIDE MY OWN CALAMITOUS HEAD, WAS A FEAR-FILLED
MESS OF CLUMSINESS
I COULD HAVE STAYED IN BED INSTEAD

BUT I FELT COMPELLED TO STRETCH AND YELL
TO TRY TO MAKE SOMETHING OUT OF MYSELF
EVEN IF IT RUINS ME
EVEN IF I MUTINY AGAINST MYSELF
AT A LATER DATE

SOMETIMES IT FEELS AN AWFUL LOT LIKE FATE
BUT NOT RIGHT NOW, IT'S JUST A MIGRAINE

IT WILL PASS

THE MIGRAINE, AND THE EMPTINESS

IT WILL SINK AWAY
IF YOU LET IT

                    MUSE
         Are you there?

                    MUSE
              (after a pause)
         Can you hear me?

it's not always people you lose.
when the flood comes,
it comes for everything.

okay   fine   shower with the lights off
hold your breath underwater
set your old photos on fire in the backyard   hibernate
bury some ashes   dig yourself up   be a dog with a bone
be a fucking bitch to everyone you know   and then
stop   and then apologize   and try something else
        maybe now you're really into tarot cards
that could be something   download an app that tells
you the moon phases   set your unholy intentions
        manifest a manageable life
        pack up and move   yes now
time to go somewhere new   right?   new is always better
        try   smiling at yourself in the mirror   try
eating your way into a better life   hungry caterpillar
your way through all those end of the world supplies
    or don't   maybe don't   maybe try something new
        yoga   just kidding not yoga   maybe vitamins
        wait we could try veganism again instead
oh or what if you chase your own tail
chase someone else's tail   chase something to fill up
the fucking quiet in your goddamn house   pick a vice
        then pick three more for good measure
        carve the world up with a kitchen knife
fall in love with your nemesis   kiss your knuckles
        drink cheap wine for dinner again even though you
know it won't fix anything and
        may in fact make everything   worse
listen to your friend's new sobriety podcast   join tiktok
    you have to try   something is going to keep you alive
pull your hair out trying to find it   set the world alight to
    keep yourself warm   do   whatever you   must

You're treading water. You've been doing it as
long as you can remember but you're rarely aware of it.
It's second nature at this point. You're used to the sore
muscles. You made friends with the fish. You're tired a lot
but you assume everyone else is tired a lot too. And you
sink sometimes, sure. You fall asleep and wake up
choking a little. You thrash around, but you work it out
eventually. You get your head above the surface and you
gulp in air so fast it hurts your chest. And then there you
are, treading water again. Paddling around. Happy as a
dog that doesn't know better.

One day you're complaining about the exhaustion
and your friend says, *what are you talking about? There's a
ladder right over there. Just get out and dry off.*

But

you don't understand.
And you're scared of what's over there.
You've got no idea what it feels like

to stand
on two feet.

You don't remember

not
being

in the water.

for myself, when i want to die

there are trees still,
and you love those.
the smell of dirt and pine.
sunshine on bare skin
almost feels like being touched
if you close your eyes.
the cat sleeps on your chest
to hear the sound of your heartbeat
and she'd miss that.
one day when your brain is calmer
you might be able to read books again.
there are people who love you
even if they don't really know you.
that doesn't always have to be a burden
or a wound.
it still feels good to write poems
if you don't show them to anyone.
it will not always be like this.
you don't have to believe that
but you have to believe something.

if my grief is proof that you existed,
how do I ever let myself stop feeling it?

I DO HOLD ONTO IT.
I DO HOLD ONTO IT.
I DO HOLD ONTO IT.
I DO HOLD ONTO IT.
I DO HOLD ONTO IT.
I DO HOLD ONTO IT.
I DO HOLD ONTO IT.
I DO HOLD ONTO IT.
I DO HOLD ONTO IT.
I DO HOLD ONTO IT.
I DO HOLD ONTO IT.
I DO HOLD ONTO IT.
I DO HOLD ONTO IT.
I DO HOLD ONTO IT AND THEN

one day, after I have spoken it enough / after I have held it enough /
after I have written it down enough / memorialized it enough /
treasured it / despised it / relied on it / forgotten it / remembered it
and chastised myself for the forgetting / one day, after I have worn
the face of grief for so long that I stop recognizing myself / after grief
no longer sounds like a real word / after I have finished the hard
work / the labor of sadness / one day,   after

I LOOSEN MY GRIP.

it's easy to get stuck hurting

Pain is indiscriminately sticky. It clings to everything. It smells familiar. I understand why people lay down inside of it and refuse to get up. I have spent my own years in that hole. Even called it a home.

Promise me you won't make a safe place of your suffering. That you won't return to it on purpose. That you won't make nice with it. Pain is a teacher but it is not a friend.

MUSE
I know it's hard right now. The
whole world is scrambling to put
itself back together and you're
scared. Scared things could get
bad again. Scared things aren't
finished being bad yet. Sure the
world didn't end yesterday or
last week but it still might
tomorrow. Joy and hope feel so
far away at times, you're not
sure they're ever coming back.
And you've been feeling this way
for so long, you're starting to
think maybe peace and happiness
weren't meant for someone like
you. But you're wrong.

(POET shrugs.)

MUSE
You're going to be happy again.
Your own delight is going to
catch you so off guard one day. I
don't know when it'll happen or
how long it'll take but that
future where you're loved and
joyous, it's waiting for you. And
it's content to wait. You don't
need to go chasing it down right
now. It'll find you. All you have
to do now is rest. Breathe. Tend
to yourself. You'll find your way
home.

THERE IS A PERIOD OF REST NECESSARY FOR EVERYTHING

the poetry book speaks

haven't we all been hurt
in a way worth talking about

just a little

between friends?

the open notebook speaks

you want a place to belong, honey?
pick up a pen and come home

to a young poet,

There's something I need you to remember. I'm reminding you because I forget. I forget all the time.

Your worth is not determined by how well you can speak about your trauma / how pretty you can package it / how many metaphors you can make about suffering. I know it's tempting to write with your own blood but you don't need to. I know it feels good to hang your wounds up on the wall for a while but you don't need to. And you can take them down if you change your mind. You can throw them out whenever you want. Whether necessary or unnecessary, you can start over whenever you feel like it. You owe nothing to the page or the mic or the readers or the scorekeepers. Not your privacy or your honesty or your trauma or your sadness or your tongue. You can share them but you don't have to. You are not writing yourself into a box. And if you feel like you are, you can erase the lines. Or draw a lid. Lift it up and walk out. Poetry can be a bruise as much as it can be a bandage. You don't have to keep pressing the hurt.

So we're living in the future
and it isn't beautiful.

Not yet, anyway.
It needs tending to.

Righteous anger
and unyielding empathy.

There is no more time
for waiting.

The future is here
wailing like a newborn

and it demands
sacrifice from us all.

GIVE ME A REASON
GIVE ME A REASON NOT TO RUN
YOU KNOW THAT WE WEREN'T MADE FOR THIS
I COULD SIT IN THE SUN
INSTEAD OF SOBBING 9 TO 5
MAKING MONEY FOR SOMEONE
WHO DOESN'T GIVE A SHIT IF I SURVIVE
AS LONG AS ALL THE WORK GETS DONE

aren't you tired of being polite
don't you want to lose it, just a little
just enough
to raise a fuss
just enough
to inconvenience
the cruel hand of fate
which keeps twisting its knife into your side
whether you bear it quietly
or not

THERE IS SO
LITTLE IN THIS
LIFE YOU ALONE
CAN CONTROL

BUT YOUR VOICE
CAN BE A
POWERFUL TOOL
FOR CHANGE
WHEN ADDED
TO A CHORUS
OF OTHERS.

~~THE GREAT GATSBY~~

girl

from

nowhere

with a   distaste for
large parties
small parties
the boom of a bass drum,
suddenly

h a t e s

introvert
lonely

standing alone

I am clinging to joy this year
small joy and ugly joy
any shiny pretty thing that makes me feel alive

yeah i'm here
again.
foolish i guess
but that's not new.
and you   are my oldest friend.
and one time   you called me a peach
and then i wrote it
into all of my poems
          like a callback
          or a crumb trail.
my overused metaphor.
my overripe want.

i don't know.
i loved you for eleven years
and i never was sorry for it.

i'm still not.

rough draft

everything looks so bleak and now more than ever
I feel you like a tiny tide in my chest / no
you are a moon and I'm trapped in your glow / no
I am water and you pull me to you constantly
moon-struck / wait that doesn't make fucking sense
love and poetry are similar that way
they don't always have to
but I'm trying to
I'm trying
I'm trying to say that everything is shit
and I'm tired of not kissing you

Yes it's true, the horrible things remain horrible
and even your mother won't always agree with you
and the weather is so heavy
all it does is remind you that you're not being touched.

I agree, the news is too ugly to watch today
and yes I know people have been cruel without reason
and your heart is hurting still
from things you won't tell your friends about.

I know.
I know.

I know it doesn't make it better that I know.
It is one thing to be seen
and another thing entirely to be held.

Drove up the road
the first time in months,
everything looked different.
It seems these days I blink
and life goes on without permission.
But I remember sitting us
in the bed of her father's truck.
Her finger hooked deep inside my mouth.
Fish already on the line
and scared of getting caught.
Now there's a new grocery store
in our old abandoned lot.
And all the love we hid in it
is really mostly gone.
The landscape of our love affair
has permanently shifted.
Despite the way that stings me still
I offer no resistance.

I HELD MY OWN HAND
BECAUSE I DESERVE IT
THESE DAYS I TOUCH MY BODY
MORE THAN HE DOES
'CAUSE I WON'T HURT IT

to the person listening to "moon song" by phoebe bridgers on repeat:

love will not always feel this way.
the dark blue of it all.
the sinking.
it won't always have you by the throat like that.

The sun is gone but other things remain for now. Holiday string lights on windows across the street. Flurries melting on the asphalt. I've become one of those nosy people, eyes glued to the window. Our neighbors had seven guests over last night. Plus five usual residents. Each of them maskless and laughing. I don't really understand how people can do that anymore. There have been so many ways to lose someone this year. There were so many things I didn't expect to lose. I have known better winters than this one but at least I made it to winter. Pity to have your life and still not be thankful for it. I am trying to want to find a way forward.

When you lead the reader into the dark,
you have to lead them back out,
I say.
I say this in some other time.
In fact,
this is an echo.
Something left over from a different year
full of more manageable catastrophes.
But I say it.
I make it a rule.
Live by it.
Demand it of myself as a writer.
So what now?
Someone is waiting for me to take their hand
and tell them everything is going to be fine.
But it's not going to be fine,
is it?
You're in the quicksand with me.
You're under water.
You're burning up.
I don't have to tell you about suffering.
You already know.
You're the one in this pit
with enough light to read by.
Can't you show me
the way out?

I need to lean against the shoulder of a good friend.

What was I doing again?

I am no longer sure if I exist in the same reality as everyone around me.   I am no longer sure of most things.

There is too much to do.

I've been alone so long I can't remember which conversations are the real ones.

I feel hollow as a bird bone and just as easy to break.

oh, to live unremarkably

if I have children,
I hope they live quiet lives.
no fires for them.
no sickness.
no breaking news stories.
I hope they die of old age,
far from the pages of history books.

making peace

Grief returns, though I have banished it. Grief doesn't listen to logic or reason. Never waits for an invitation either. It's impatient. Grief tugs on my sleeve in the middle of dinner. It begs for attention. Grief asks to be fed, asks to be picked up, asks to be tucked in at night. Grief wears a face I don't recognize but that doesn't mean it isn't my face. Grief paints the walls blue. It sneaks out onto the roof and just lays there for long stretches of time. Grief buys me a parting gift and promises to visit again soon. I say, *you know where to find me.* And it says, *yes. I do.*

If you ever know love intimately,
you will know grief intimately.
You will be struck
by deep moments
of profound sadness.
You will,
at some point,
wade through the waters of despair.
I hope you're braver for it.
I hope it makes you love harder.

DON'T BE AFRAID TO
PEEL YOUR CLEMENTINE-HEART

IT'S OKAY TO HAND THE PIECES
OUT TO STRANGERS

I'M REACHING OUT
TOWARD YOU TODAY
AND WHEREVER YOU
ARE, I HOPE YOU
CAN FEEL IT.

I HOPE YOU'RE
REACHING
BACK TOO.

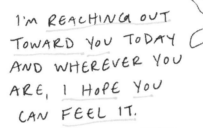

the love poem

tear this page from its book
shove it in my face if I ever say otherwise

I was bleeding for you right here
and this is proof

You're glowing, baby.
You're a bad fucking bitch.
You could be the queen of hell if you wanted.
You could kiss the throat of heaven.
Stick your unholy tongue in its mouth
and laugh your mad head right off.
Love is an act of creation
and you are the creator.
Wrap it in gold and ribbon.
Gift it to yourself.

there are many days I forget to be kind to myself
but this will not be one

LOOK AT YOU, LITTLE REVOLUTIONARY

DEFYING THE WILL OF YOUR BRAIN
THE GREAT DECIEVER

YOUR GOVERNMENT
AND THOSE RUBBER BULLETS
AIMED AT YOUR HEAD

ALL THE MARKETING EXECS
WHO WANT YOU TO HATE
YOURSELF

AND WHATEVER ELSE WANTS
YOU DOWN AND OUT

YOUR SURVIVAL
IS AN ACT OF RESISTANCE

I WOULD CALL YOU UP
JUST TO TALK ABOUT
THE MOON

MUSE
You sound like you have your head
above water today.

POET
Maybe. But the sadness is going
to come back and that hole in the
floor is going to open up and I'm
going to fall into it again. I'm
going to be underwater for so
long.

MUSE
There is the constant risk of
another loss to mourn, another
government failure, another month
of despair around the corner. But
you always find your way back to
the surface.

POET
(after a pause)
I'm tired of finding my way back.
It is exhausting to want to be
okay. To want to be alive. To
want the world to be better than
it is.

new normal

I still get so overwhelmed
by the news

that I burst into tears
once (or twice) a day

and then I go back
to whatever I was doing

like nothing happened;
it's just part of the routine.

years from now
I will wake up
in another place
and for a sharp
panicked moment
there in the dark
I will think
that I'm back
in this room.

I am   friends with my alone.   It asks   nothing
of me.   It gives me my privacy.   I stretch   out

in bed and kick into no one. I read   when I want
to read   and I cook when I want to cook   and I

watch what I want to watch.   I don't need someone
next to me just to fill up space in   the room.

I'm at the bottom of the barrel of my lonely.
There's so little left to say about it.

Absence is

still
after all of this

just absence.

pandemic dreams in pieces

everyone is shouting at

our politicians, who squabble over which of us mice
deserve a few crumbs of old bread. nobody asked for old
bread

but Xena: Warrior Princess is fighting a white supremacist
to the death and she's doing it in front of everyone

and then I wonder if I will ever accept good love but it
looks like the jury's still out on that one plus I'm stuck in
the middle of the ocean anyway so like

I do kinda think pirates had the right idea, living like
that. I too, would love to stab someone right now

a quick jab right in the shoulder

look at all this blood.
it's coming down in buckets, like rain

is that a cough or a nest of spiders in the throat

you reach out and you rip me open just like that. My bad,

phone sex at the end of the world

There is still sickness outside
and fire too, again
death and the shouting downstairs

but after a chorus of your moaning
and my heavy breathing,
I curl onto my side
peeling the wet sheet from the back of my thighs
and think, *this is the happiest I've been in months.*

The call ends and still,
I lay like that   for hours.

Once there was a girl swallowed up by a big fish. She never panicked. Lived her life in there like it was normal. She disappeared day by day and she welcomed it. She never knew anything different.

Once there was nobody. And the moss crept. And the trees grew. And the skies cleared. And everything was so lonely.

Once there was a person treading water. They thought about drowning for the longest time.

BLESS THE FRIENDS
YOU CAN FUCK UP WITH

BLESS THE PLAYLISTS
AND LONG DRIVES

BLESS THE POETS
YOU GREW UP WITH

BLESS THE ART
THAT KEPT YOU ALIVE

LONG ENOUGH
TO FIGURE OUT

THAT YOU EVEN WANTED
TO SURVIVE

It's a long road to walk and you don't have a choice. There are no other roads. You're wandering the dystopian future and you're thirsty all the time. Your bag is too heavy so you put some things down and keep walking. You don't look back. You leave some unread text messages, the emails, a friendship, one or two memories, a little bit of joy. You keep going because you have to keep going because what else is there to do but keep going? So you walk more. And your mouth gets drier and the sun gets hotter and you get tired. So tired. You're tired all the time, actually. Even when you sleep. Even when you sit by the roadside for a minute. You never catch your breath. There's no time. You do what anyone would do in your situation. You leave more things behind. Good hygiene and the laundry and all the dishes.

You walk so slowly sometimes you don't feel like you're moving at all. One foot in front of the other. And one morning you roll over wide awake. You dig around for reasons to keep going but you can't find any. You still get up. You're used to the rhythm now. The pace. You get nervous when you're not on the move. Your bag is too heavy. Too much to carry. You're always carrying too much. You've been dragging it in the dirt behind you for weeks and you can't remember why. What's in it that's so important? You don't have enough energy to check. So you leave it. Right there in the dirt. And sure, you make it. You reach a house one day and you go inside and you sit down and say, *I'm here.* The owner of the house doesn't recognize you anymore but they let you stay anyway. They can see you've been through a lot. And you have been. Survival demanded so much of you. You don't even know what you've lost.

we are, all of us
all of us left
going someplace new

i hope it is a good place
i hope to see your face there

You meet yourself
in a dark room
when all the noise
has died down.

You reject yourself
or you hold yourself close.

Those are
the only options.

I made meringues
stiff peaks of egg and sugar
I hovered around the oven for two hours
waiting for them to dry out
and then I feasted in my underwear
on the couch

and I thought you know
I'm not very good at wanting to be alive
but I am very good at waiting

thank fuck for that

new horrible things every day
so i crave sameness
the reliable comfort of familiarity
i ask the universe for a constant
and it hands me: grief
i return it
i ask the universe for a constant
and it hands me: ache
i return it
i ask the universe for a constant
and it hands me: myself

I crawled
on broken glass
to get here.
You better believe
I'm living it up.
I will swallow stars
if I want to.
May my dreams come true.
May my enemies eat shit.
Times are tough
but I'm a fucking nightmare.
I have my boot
on the throat of hell
right now.
Watch me beat my demons
into submission.
Surviving's ugly work
and here I am,
so hideously alive.

you can't kill your old self but you can try
you can't kill your old self but you can leave it behind
you can walk out on yourself whenever you want
go ahead
be unfaithful to yourself
grab the good shit and leave
it's not you
it's me

new year

we have done it
waded through another impossible year
stared failure in the face and cruelty too
we did not always plan to make it
but look at us
survivors nonetheless

I cannot write a poem that will fix the world
but I can write a poem that will make me want to stay in it
a moment longer

and then I can write another.

I'm so sorry. No, listen.

Hear me, not as some disembodied voice from a stranger's tongue. Hear me as if I am next to you. Hear me as you hear a loved one calling from very far away.

I miss you.

I love you.

I know it has not been easy. Believe me. Day in and day out. You have suffered more than you've said, I know it. I see it on you, like a weight. I see it on both of us. We are different than we were before. Angrier. Harder.

You don't have to exist in survival mode with me. You're okay. Your strength is unparalleled and your resiliency is inspiring, but they're not necessary here. Leave them by the door with your shoes. Drag your body in here and rest with me. Grieve whatever you must, however you must.

Let me hold you while there is still something of us left.

You're trapped in an exhausting life, in a dangerous world which has resisted most efforts to change it. Everything feels out of your control. The suffering around you is relentless and often meaningless. The trauma is inescapable. Your hopelessness is not a personal failing. You have no hope because the world stripped it away from you one broken promise at a time. Every day wears you down and makes you feel like less of yourself and it's not even your fault.

So, okay. Okay. You hang your head. You disconnect. You turn inward. You bury yourself in comforts and try to live a quiet life with your back turned to the world but the world refuses to leave you be. It doesn't want you well-rested. It wants you on edge and burnt out. Too tired to do anything about anything.

You can stay like that. I understand why people do.

Or you can try to step out here and be part of something. You can chase the things that make you feel bigger than yourself. Passions. Connection. Community. Love.

The world can strip everything else away
and you'll still have love.

Sure, love is soft and love is vulnerable and love is tender and everything else—but love is hard too. Angry too. Protective and defensive and sometimes even ugly. Love is standing up for other people, lifting the voices of other people, having the backs of other people. Love is not just wanting the best for everyone but working toward it. Taking actionable steps. Putting your body in front of someone else's body. Love is being afraid of saying the wrong thing but still saying something. Love is showing up and showing out for the people that you care about. Love is expanding the circle of people that you care about. Love is looking inward, healing and thriving and living—

but looking outward too.

Seeing what needs help growing there.
Asking how you can best lend a hand.

one day there will be joy again
and I will rise to meet it.

Your existence causes ripples in the world.
Like a stone into a lake.
Your little waves.
Reaching and reaching.
Everything is touched by you.
The frog and the crawdad,
fish and mud,
the heron,
the reed grass.
And if everything is touched by you,
can you ever be truly alone?
You are hands-open, reaching and reaching.
Everything under the sun
is reaching and reaching right back.

Your hands are in my mouth. In my hair. In my chest cavity. I'm touching you even when I'm not touching you. I love the body even as it breaks down. We are both in pre-existing condition which I think is the state of a dream. Ephemeral and easy to forget.

So we're in the dream and I've brought up the end of the world. I say, *it's standing on our doorstep. It's right out there. Look at it.*

And you say, *the world is not ending. It's time to wake up. I can't wait to see you. I've missed you so much.*

my dearest friend —

your love,
like all good love,
sustains me. ♡

self-soothing

You are enough.
Your life is worth living.
People love you deeply.
Your existence is, itself, a wonder.
A miracle you're even here
speaking to whomever you're speaking to,
hurting however you're hurting,
laughing over whatever.
You series of unlikely events.
You star-hearted little fiend.
You've made a mess of everything.
That's part of being alive.
Now we will fix it.
Which is also part of being alive.
You're doing just fine.

NOT SURE WHO I AM ANYMORE
WHEN I'M NOT HURTING
BUT I OWE IT TO MYSELF TO TRY
AND DO A LITTLE LEARNING

INT. BEDROOM — NIGHT

POET's laptop is balanced on some pillows,
open to a word document. The cursor is
blinking back at her. She sits cross-legged
in bed with a water bottle between her legs
and headphones shoved into her ears to block
the noise downstairs. She is typing and
deleting. Typing and deleting.

The bed starts vibrating. Her phone is going
off, lost somewhere under a heap of blankets
and pillows. She rips out the headphones,
rescues the phone, and brings it to her ear.

> **MUSE**
> What is this, draft forty-seven?

> **POET**
> (sighs)
> I'm struggling with the ending. I
> mean, I'm ready for it to be
> finished but it feels wrong to
> end something that isn't over.

> **MUSE**
> So don't end it. Nothing else has
> ended. There is still loss out
> there, danger and illness and
> despair. All of this persists, so
> too must we.

> **POET**
> What then, instead of an ending?

> **MUSE**
> A pause. A promise to return.

poetry and other vices

I can no longer separate
the work of poetry-making
from the work of being alive.
The poems are evidence
that I still care enough about my life
to write some of it down.

before you leave

I spent years of my life
writing poems in the dark.
I was just lonely
until I had a reader.
Then I was a poet.

That's what you did for me.

Thank you for being here.

Thank you for being here with me.

when you are finished with the work of being sad
when you have cried all of your crying
broken your promises
romanticized the end of your life
reached for whatever you reach for

when you are finished with the work of being sad
come with me
somewhere the sun is rising
and it is time to begin again

If you enjoyed this book, please consider:
-leaving a brief review on amazon
-reading or sharing the book on tiktok
-adding it to shelves on goodreads
-requesting it at your local library or bookstore
-sharing photos of the book/poems on instagram
-suggesting or passing it along to a friend
-sending me an interview or podcast request
-connecting with me @tristamateer on tiktok or ig
-signing up for the newsletter on my website for updates
        tristamateer.com
-following my patreon for early content and exclusive work
        patreon.com/tristamateer

You all do so much by even picking these books up that I hate to ask for more but I get a lot of messages from readers about how they can support my work and these are the most helpful ways! Thank you for helping this little book reach the people who might need it. I know that these actions seem small on their own but they really do add up and I appreciate the effort so much!!!

a note from the author

This is not intended to be an extensive account of our global crisis or a universal story. It's not one. I'm a white American with pre-existing mental/physical health issues, who was living in the USA at the time I was writing these pieces. I expect its content reflects that.

Here's your additional obligatory note that poetry is not a substitute for proper mental healthcare! (However if you, like me, find "proper mental healthcare" hard to access, poetry can be helpful in the same way that journaling is.)

I also want to be perfectly clear: protests against systemic racism and police brutality were a huge, necessary part of our year here. With that said, I obviously did not want to publish work that would profit off of the suffering and trauma of Black folks. For that reason, you did not find overt poems specifically about racism or the Black Lives Matter movement in this book. If you're looking for pieces like that, I implore you to check out the Black poets who have been writing on these topics for years. Claudia Rankine, Danez Smith, and Jericho Brown in particular come to mind.

As always, thank you for reading.

Trista Mateer

about the author

Trista Mateer is a queer visual artist and poet from Maryland. You may recognize her as the author of such poetry collections as *When the Stars Wrote Back* (Random House Children's) or *Aphrodite Made Me Do It* (Central Avenue) etc. You may not. That's okay. You can keep up with her on TikTok, Instagram, and Twitter @tristamateer.

more info: tristamateer.com
merch shop: etsy.com/shop/tristamateershop

If you loved *girl, isolated*...
try Trista Mateer's other books: *When the Stars Wrote Back, Aphrodite Made Me Do It, Honeybee,* and *The Dogs I Have Kissed.*

Acknowledgements...
You know what, this section is short because I didn't speak to people this year. I sat at home and cried and texted Nikita a hundred times a day so thank you Nikita Gill. Caitlyn Siehl, Natalie Noland, Caitlin Conlon, Zane Frederick, & Summer Webb were also forced to read this book between one and six times apiece so I could pick their brains. This book would not exist without their input. And yes, the title is very much a reference to Girl, Interrupted by Susanna Kaysen!

Here's to... hanging in there.

57117184R10106